THE FALL OF
MEXICO CITY

THE FALL OF MEXICO CITY

George Ochoa

Silver Burdett Press
Englewood Cliffs, New Jersey

Acknowledgments

The author thanks Melinda Corey and Jacqueline Ogburn for their invaluable assistance in reviewing and editing the manuscript.

Consultants:

We thank the following people for reviewing the manuscript and offering their helpful suggestions:

Julian Nava
Historian
Former U.S. Ambassador to Mexico

Gloria Contreras
Professor
College of Education
North Texas State University

Cover, title page, and contents page illustrations courtesy of the Library of Congress.

Library of Congress Cataloging-in-Publication Data

Ochoa, George.
    The fall of Mexico City / by George Ochoa.
        p.   cm.—(Turning points in American history)
    Bibliography: p.
    Includes index.
    1. Mexico City (Mexico) History—American occupation, 1847-1848—
Juvenile literature. I. Title. II. Series.
    E406.M6037 1989   89-6146
    973'.05—dc20   CIP
      ISBN 0-382-09853-6 (pbk.) ISBN 0-382-09836-6   AC
(lib. bdg.)

Editorial coordination by Richard G. Gallin

 Created by Media Projects Incorporated

C. Carter Smith, *Executive Editor*
Toni Rachiele, *Managing Editor*
Charles Wills, *Project Editor*
Bernard Schleifer, *Design Consultant*
Simon Hu, *Cartographer*

Manufactured in the United States of America.

ISBN 0-382-09836-6 [lib. bdg.]
10 9 8 7 6 5 4 3 2 1

ISBN 0-382-09853-6 [pbk.]
10 9 8 7 6 5 4 3 2 1

CONTENTS

INTRODUCTION

THE CONQUERORS

At daybreak on September 14, 1847, American soldiers saw the white flag of truce flying from the citadel that guarded Mexico City. For the first time in history, the United States had forced the surrender of a foreign capital.

The Americans trudged into the fallen city, weary from weeks of fighting. They were covered with mud from camping on wet ground. Many were wounded and limping. Lieutenant P.G.T. Beauregard, one of the officers, described the sight as "anything but glorious in appearance . . . whatever history may say."

The soldiers raised the American flag over the Palace of the Moctezumas—so called for the Aztec kings who had ruled this city hundreds of years earlier. The soldiers took over the Grand Plaza and waited for their commander. Soon he rode in. General Winfield Scott—

American troops enter Mexico City's central plaza on September 18, 1847.

brightly uniformed and escorted by horsemen with flashing swords—was cheered by his troops.

The cheers were well deserved. Scott had led his men to a victory many had thought impossible. His troops, outnumbered by the enemy, had fought for six months deep inside Mexico. He had lacked the full support of the American president and at one point was forced to send home many of his men. Even so, Scott had captured Mexico City and virtually brought an end to the Mexican War.

Virtually—but not quite. Although the Mexican army had abandoned the city, ordinary citizens were determined to fight back. Within an hour after Scott rode into the city, shots were fired at the Americans. Rioting spread. From windows and rooftops, snipers shot at soldiers; those without guns threw bottles and stones. Poorly armed civilians fought armed patrols in the streets. Not for three days did the Americans gain

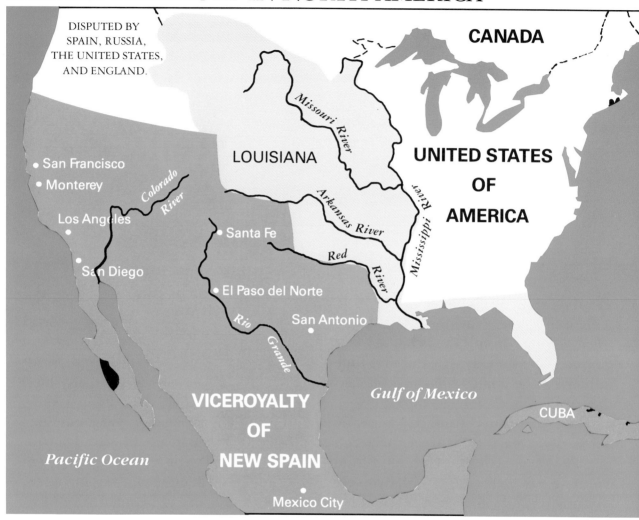

DISPUTED BY
SPAIN, RUSSIA,
THE UNITED STATES,
AND ENGLAND.

CANADA

Missouri River

LOUISIANA

UNITED STATES
OF
AMERICA

• San Francisco
• Monterey

Colorado River

Los Angeles

Arkansas River

• Santa Fe

Mississippi River

Red River

• San Diego

• El Paso del Norte

San Antonio

Rio Grande

VICEROYALTY
OF
NEW SPAIN

Gulf of Mexico

CUBA

Pacific Ocean

• Mexico City

control. But they did gain control, and the Mexican War was won.

The war had turned out to be an enormous success for the United States. In the seventeen months between the first shot on the Rio Grande and the fall of Mexico City, American forces had won a string of victories against a confident army that greatly outnumbered them. The victories were paid for by the lives of about 13,000 Americans—1,733 killed on the battlefield; most of the rest killed by disease.

The greatest fruit of victory was land: nearly 2 million square miles of land that was formerly part of Mexico. This included what is now Texas, California, Nevada, and Utah; most of Arizona and New Mexico; and parts of Colorado, Wyoming, Kansas, and Oklahoma. In decades to come, the settlement of that land would bring great benefits for the growing nation. But despite those benefits, the Mexican War is today poorly remembered.

One reason Americans tend to forget the Mexican War is that another conflict overshadowed it thirteen years later—the Civil War. Another reason is that many people, both at the time and since, have seen the Mexican War as unjust, provoked by the United States in order to gain the land it wanted. The war laid a poor foundation for relations with Mexico and the rest of Latin America. Today, many Mexican Americans, or Chicanos, in the American Southwest still think of that part of the country as "the lost land."

The story of the Mexican War is a story of fierce battle, political intrigue, and the popular dream of "manifest destiny"—America's belief that it was destined by God to spread across the continent. It is also the story of a moral debate on the use of American power that is still going on today. The debate is perhaps best symbolized by the American flag flying for the first time over the capital of another nation.

1

THE FAR NORTH

In capturing Mexico City, General Scott had followed the invasion route of another successful conqueror—the Spanish conquistador Hernán Cortés. Over 300 years earlier, Cortés's attack through the same hills and marshes destroyed an ancient civilization and marked the beginning of modern Mexican history.

Cortés and his 550 men landed in 1519 on the coast of the Gulf of Mexico near Veracruz. They came without the consent of the king of Spain to look for gold. They found it, but it belonged to someone else—a people called the Aztecs, or Mexicas. The Aztec empire was hundreds of years old and, ruled by a king named Moctezuma, governed millions of people. In two and a half years, through treachery, warfare, and the help of Native American allies, Cortés gained control of the empire.

A Spanish conquistador—one of the men who turned the Aztec empire into a colony of Spain.

Moctezuma's capital city, renamed Mexico City, became the capital of New Spain. The colony was ruled by a viceroy, or representative of the king. Spanish customs became dominant, but the native culture did not completely disappear. Basic food crops like corn and beans continued to be grown. The Native Americans hid figurines of their gods and goddesses inside the statues of Roman Catholic saints.

The Spanish did introduce changes, however. Native Americans were put to work mining gold and silver to send back to Spain. Spanish owners of large plantations grew crops like tobacco, coffee, and sugar cane, since these could be sold in Europe at a profit. The peasant farmers, known as peons, were kept in debt to large landowners, and were not much better off than slaves.

Unlike the British colonists who settled North America, the Spanish married freely with the Native Americans. A mix of Spanish and Indian physical characteristics, known as *mes-*

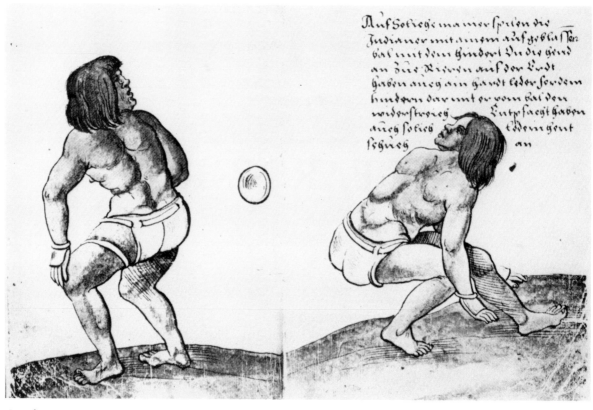

Cortés brought two Aztecs back to Spain. A contemporary drawing shows the two playing a ball game.

tizo, became common in New Spain. People of pure Spanish descent, however, continued to own much of the property. A bishop in 1800 wrote, "The Spaniards comprise a tenth of the total population, and they alone hold almost all the property and wealth of the realm."

New Spain outgrew the farthest reaches of the Aztec empire. It gained control of what is now Mexico and eventually most of Central America. It also expanded into the area that is now the southwestern United States—the region over which the Mexican War would be fought.

That region—the "Far North" to the Spanish—stretched from California to Texas, from the Great Salt Lake to the Rio Grande. It was a country of richness and variety. California, on the coast of the Pacific Ocean, featured vast forests and rich valleys and mountains. The lands that are now Arizona and New Mexico contained deserts, mesas (plateaus), and the many-colored walls of the Grand Canyon. What is now Texas ranged from the moist plains of the Gulf of Mexico to forests, deserts, and prairies grazed by bison.

The native cultures of the "Far North" were as varied as the land. Some were grouped by the Spanish under the general name of "Pueblo" or village, because of the flat-roofed, many-roomed structures in which they lived. The Pueblos, who included groups like the Hopis and Tewas, were peaceful corn farmers skilled in weaving and pottery. Also in the region were the Apaches, fierce warriors and hunters; and the Navajos, who combined hunting with agriculture. They and the many other tribes of the Far North shared a belief in the sacredness of the land, expressed in poetry and ritual.

These Native Americans were bound to come into conflict with the Spanish, who arrived seeking gold and magical cities. Explorers like Francisco Vásquez de Coronado in the 1540s were disappointed not to find anything like the fabled "Seven Cities of Gold." The dis-appointment kept New Spain from settling the Far North for about fifty years. Then the government began to worry that other European countries would move in unless the Spanish did.

In 1609 the mission of Santa Fe was founded in what is today New Mexico. Other settlements in the Far North followed, including San Antonio, Texas, in 1718, and San Diego, California, in 1769. The Spanish also spread to more eastern parts of what is today the United States. The city of St. Augustine, Florida, was founded by the Spanish in 1565. The southernmost parts of what are now Alabama and Mississippi were held by Spain. Spain also possessed the Louisiana Territory from 1763 until 1800, when the region was ceded to the French.

Most Spanish settlements sprang up

Missions—local churches—were a symbol of the Spanish presence in the Southwest.

Mexican settlers in California dance the fandango, a traditional dance.

around the work of Roman Catholic missionary priests trying to convert the Native Americans. A garrison of soldiers would protect the local mission, and settlers were attracted by offers of land.

The Spanish settlers treated the Native American people harshly, and these people at times fought back. In 1680 the Pueblos revolted and drove the Spanish out of New Mexico. Not until 1692 did New Spain reconquer the province.

Raids by Native American tribes like the Apaches helped to keep settlers out of the Far North. In 1810 New Mexico had only about 35,000 Spanish and *mestizo* settlers. They were outnumbered by perhaps 50,000 American Indians. Texas was even more sparsely colonized, with fewer than 4,000 settlers from New Spain. It was the weakness of the Spanish hold on Texas that set the stage for war between the United States and Mexico.

In 1800 the United States was a young, small country, no more than 800 miles wide east to west, with a constitution only eleven years old. With the purchase of the Louisiana Territory from the French in 1803, the United States became, in some places, 1,000 miles wider. It also gained a border with New Spain that would become a place of conflict—the border between Louisiana and Texas.

It seemed for a time that New Spain and the United States would be able to live in harmony. The Adams-Onis

Treaty of 1819 settled various land disputes, including the question of who owned Texas. The United States agreed that Spain owned Texas, and Spain sold its territory east of the Mississippi River, including what is now Florida, to the United States.

Spain was more worried about the British and French than about the Americans, fearing that the European powers would try to take control of Texas unless more settlers could be attracted there. For that reason, the rulers of New Spain were ready to accept the offer of an American businessman to bring American colonists into Texas. That fateful decision would eventually lead to the Texan Revolution.

The American who offered to bring in the settlers was Moses Austin of Connecticut. Austin was about sixty years old. He was a former merchant, miner, and banker, and had once been a Spanish subject. In 1821 New Spain gave him an *empresario* land grant. That meant he would receive 200,000 acres in Texas if he could bring in three hundred families to settle it—all Catholic or willing to convert, and all swearing loyalty to Spain.

Austin died before he could fulfill the bargain. His son, Stephen Austin, a gentle and serious young man, took on the job. In 1823 young Austin brought the first three hundred American families to the rich coastal plain of Texas. All pledged loyalty to Mexico as new citizens. By that time, however, Mexico was no longer part of New Spain. Mex-

Stephen Austin began the American settlement of Texas in 1823.

ico City became the capital of a new country in 1824.

In 1821, the year Moses Austin died, Spanish rule was overthrown in Mexico. In fact, by 1822 all of Spain's colonies in Central and South America had become independent. The United States recognized the new governments. The Monroe Doctrine of 1823 warned Europe not to interfere with their "free and independent condition."

At the same time, Americans were suspicious of the new regimes. John Quincy Adams said that the new governments had inherited Spanish traditions of "arbitrary power" and "civil dissension." He believed that frequent rebellion and the use of military rule would make it hard for the countries to form "free or liberal institutions."

Indeed, Mexico remained stormy for years. One of its greatest conflicts was between rich and poor. The poor wanted social and economic justice. The rich, backed up by the official church and the military, wanted a strong government that would protect their own privileges.

Mexican independence owed something to both rich and poor. The fight for independence began with an uprising of poor *mestizos* in 1810. They were led by a priest named Father Hidalgo, who was captured and killed. But independence was not won until wealthy Mexicans became afraid of political changes in Spain. As Spain became more liberal, the conservative Mexicans worried that they would lose their place of power in the colony. They threw their support behind a rebel colonel named Agustín de Iturbide, who then became the emperor of the new monarchy of Mexico.

The monarchy did not last. Iturbide was overthrown by Mexicans who wanted a liberal, federal republic like that of the United States. The Constitution of 1824 created a government that guaranteed the rights of individuals and spread power among the Mexican states.

The "federalists," for the moment, ruled Mexico. But the "centralists"— those who wanted a strong military government in the Spanish tradition— were waiting in the wings. Americans in Texas preferred federal rule, since that form of government was closer to their own. But no matter who ruled, the government was unstable. One president after another was overthrown. Partly as a result, Americans in Texas had little respect for whoever was supposed to be governing them.

The Americans soon outnumbered the Mexicans in Texas. Some had been given grants of land; others had entered illegally. By 1830 there were perhaps 20,000 Americans in Texas, outnumbering Mexicans by at least four to one. Most were Southerners, who brought their slaves to farm cotton. Others raised cattle or traded goods. All were supposed to be Catholic and loyal to Mexico; most were so only on paper.

Too late, Mexico realized that it was losing Texas. The American settlers were governing themselves and ignoring Mexican law. More dangerous still, the United States as a whole was beginning to show an interest in the region. Two American presidents, John Quincy Adams and Andrew Jackson, attempted to buy Texas in the 1820s and 1830s. The offers were promptly refused and regarded as insults—and as signs of the growing threat from the United States.

In 1826 a group of Americans tried to found an independent "Republic of Fredonia" in eastern Texas. The revolt was quickly crushed, but it made the Mexicans worry even more. In 1829 the president of Mexico tried to make Texas less attractive to the Americans by abolishing slavery. This decree was aimed at American slaveowners in Texas, the only place in Mexico where slavery was still permitted. Slaveowners protested, and the decree was suspended.

In 1830 more legislation was passed to try to make sure that Texas remained in Mexican control. Limits were placed on American immigration, the slave trade was forbidden, and Mexicans were encouraged to settle in Texas. Texan-Americans were especially angered when Mexico stepped up enforcement of customs taxes, thereby keeping the settlers from trading freely with the United States. Stephen Austin sought some remedy through the law, but other colonists used rifles, attacking customs houses and army posts.

The unrest worsened with the arrival of rebellious colonists who were not afraid to use violence. The most famous were popular heroes—military men like Sam Houston of Tennessee, a friend of President Jackson's; James Bowie, the slave smuggler and adventurer who designed the long knife that bears his name; and Davy Crockett, the legendary frontiersman and one-time member of Congress.

Full revolt did not occur, however, until the federalists finally lost control in Mexico and a centralist president came to power. In 1835 President Antonio López de Santa Anna threw out the Constitution of 1824 and began to form a dictatorship. Santa Anna was colorful and ruthless, a skilled military leader who had the support of many wealthy Mexicans. Supporters called · him the "Napoleon of the West." Stephen Austin came to call him a "base, unprincipled, bloody monster."

The colorful frontiersman (and former congressman) Davy Crockett died at the Alamo, fighting beside 181 other Texas settlers.

Texas was one of many places in Mexico that opposed Santa Anna. Like other rebel groups, the Texas Convention—made up of Mexicans and Americans—demanded only a return to the Constitution of 1824. One of the rebels, Lorenzo de Zavala, had helped to write that constitution. But the tide of revolution soon led to another convention on March 2, 1836, which declared Texas independent. An American named David G. Burnet became president, with Zavala as vice president.

In the meantime, Texans had already gone to war. The first shot was fired on October 2, 1835, as a Mexican force tried

This painting depicts the last stand of the vastly outnumbered Texans against Santa Anna's troops.

to take possession of an old cannon that had been lent to the town of Gonzales. The Texan rebels raised a banner over the cannon: "Come and Take It." One Mexican died trying to take it; the rest were scattered. The Texans had won their first victory.

They won their second two months later in San Antonio. General Martín Cós, a brother-in-law of Santa Anna, had established his headquarters at a fortified mission called the Alamo. On December 5, 1835, 300 Texan rebels entered San Antonio. They began four days of house-to-house fighting that ended with the surrender of Cós's 1,400 Mexicans. As they watched Cós withdraw, the Texans believed themselves invincible. Many believed the war to be over. They were wrong.

Furious at the defeat, Santa Anna took personal command of the army. How large his forces were may never be known; some have said two thousand, others four or five thousand. But it is certain they outnumbered the 182 or so Texans they battled at the Alamo.

The Alamo was the turning point of the Texan Revolution. It is also one of history's great examples of how defeat can become victory. The men who gave their lives at the Alamo became the war cry for the Texans who won independence less than seven weeks later.

The battle almost didn't happen. Sam Houston, commander of the rebel forces, had ordered James Bowie to destroy the Alamo and get out before Santa Anna could arrive. Bowie disobeyed the order, and others joined him. Some came from the United States, answering appeals for help. The United States government was officially neutral, but private citizens—especially in the South—sent weapons and volunteers to Texas.

Davy Crockett and his troops from Tennessee arrived to help defend the Alamo. So did a company of "New Orleans Grays" from nearby Louisiana. Juan Seguín led a company of Mexicans fighting for the Constitution of 1824— still the rebels' stated objective. And William Travis, a South Carolina lawyer and lieutenant-colonel, took over command of the fort.

On February 23 Santa Anna arrived. The general surrounded the Alamo with lines of troops and artillery, and raised a red flag. This was the sign of "no quarter": unless the Texans surrendered immediately, they would be put to death upon being captured. Some men, women, and children left. Then the Texans answered with a cannon shell. Santa Anna began bombarding the Alamo.

The siege lasted thirteen days. On February 29, despite the overwhelming odds, 32 volunteers from the town of Gonzales chose to slip through the enemy lines and join the defenders. The group included an English shoemaker and a hatter from New York.

As the bombardment continued and the end drew near, legend has it that William Travis called his men together and drew a line in the sand. Those who were willing to fight to the death could join him on one side; the others could leave. All but one joined him. The one man who left was a French veteran who had seen war in Europe and was not willing to die in this one. It is supposedly from him that the legend has been passed on.

In any case, the defenders of the Alamo stayed. On March 6 Santa Anna broke through. The Texans killed hundreds of Mexicans; but in the end, all 182 Texan soldiers were dead. Women, children, and slaves were spared, but Santa Anna ordered the death of every captured soldier, just as he had said he would.

Santa Anna won the battle, but he lost the war. Texans and Americans alike were moved deeply by the story of the Alamo and angered by what they saw as Santa Anna's cruelty. He showed his cruelty again on March 27, when he ordered the massacre of about 300 unarmed Texan prisoners outside Goliad. Meanwhile, Sam Houston marched east with what was left of the rebel army—all of 370 men. Support for the rebels was strongest in eastern Texas, and Houston's army had grown to 783 by April.

On April 21, by the San Jacinto River, the Texans took their revenge. In a savage surprise attack on Santa Anna's army, Houston's soldiers killed 600 Mexicans and took hundreds more prisoner.

Sam Houston, though wounded, led the Texan army to victory over Santa Anna at the Battle of San Jacinto. He later became president of the Republic of Texas.

Their shout was "Remember the Alamo! Remember Goliad!" Terrified Mexicans shouted back, "Me no Alamo! Me no Goliad!" They were not heard. In 18 minutes, what was left of the Mexican army was put to flight.

Among those taken prisoner was General Santa Anna. In exchange for his freedom, the dictator signed a treaty recognizing Texan independence. This made him an object of disgust to many Mexicans, who soon drove him from power. The Congress in Mexico City rejected the treaty, saying it had been made under duress. But for the moment, with Sam Houston as its new president, Texas was a free nation. Under a flag with a single star, it was known as the Lone Star Republic.

Although the United States did not officially recognize Texas until the following year, many Americans were pleased by what had happened. Calls arose for annexation of Texas as a state. But other Americans saw Texas as a symbol not of freedom but of slavery. The economy of Texas, like that of the Southern states that were its neighbors, was based on the forced labor of blacks. To annex Texas into the Union would be to encourage slavery and give new

Lopez de Santa Anna, soldier and dictator, was defeated by Texan troops shortly after his victory at the Alamo.

power to the slave states in Congress.

The issue of whether to allow slavery to expand threatened to divide North from South, but for the moment a crisis was postponed. Efforts to annex Texas met with defeat in Congress. Mexico had warned that annexation would lead to war. Less than ten years later, it did.

2

MANIFEST DESTINY

In 1841 the Republic of Texas sent an expedition hundreds of miles west to Santa Fe, New Mexico. Santa Fe was the center of a rich trade in silver and fur. Texas hoped to gain a share in the trade—and also to convince the people of Santa Fe to revolt against Mexico. The expedition envisioned a Texan republic stretching across New Mexico all the way to California. The 300 Texans not only failed to convince anyone to revolt but were captured as invaders and marched to Mexico City. They were only released after strong American and British protests.

Mexico considered this "invasion" a sign of the continuing danger from Texas and the United States. The English-speaking people in both republics seemed altogether too interested in expanding into Mexico's Far North. Another invasion, in October 1842, drove home the point. American commodore

A poster from James K. Polk's successful presidential campaign in 1844.

Thomas Ap Catesby Jones heard a rumor that war had broken out between the United States and Mexico. He sailed at once to Monterey, California, and forced the startled Mexican garrison to surrender. The next day the commodore was embarrassed to learn that war had not broken out. He offered apologies and lowered the American flag. But the blunder increased Mexican suspicion of America's intentions.

In fact, although Commodore Jones had acted without orders, his country had long been interested in the Mexican province of California. In the 1820s President John Quincy Adams had weighed its possible value to the United States, and in the 1830s President Andrew Jackson had tried to buy it. When that failed, he suggested privately to an agent of the newly independent Texas that Texas should attempt to expand to California. Partly because of such encouragement that Texas had launched its disastrous Santa Fe expedition.

Even after that expedition, elements in both Texas and the United States kept their eyes on California. Those elements were as highly placed as President Sam Houston of Texas and President John Tyler of the United States. In 1842 Tyler's secretary of state Daniel Webster tried to obtain British help in convincing Mexico to cede California to the United States. That effort fell apart after Commodore Jones's untimely invasion of Monterey.

There were several reasons for American interest in California. One was the fear that European powers, principally Great Britain, were also interested. This fear was largely unfounded: there is no evidence that the British government planned to acquire California. In fact, Britain hoped that California would remain in Mexican hands so that it would not add to the growing strength of the United States. Nevertheless, the fear of British expansion was widely used to justify American expansion.

A more solid reason for expanding was the rich trade that California enjoyed. New England shipowners had long ago started trading American manufactured goods for California hide and tallow. Yankee whaling ships docked at the ports of Monterey and San Francisco. Goods were also exchanged with China on the other side of the Pacific Ocean. That trade expanded dramatically with an 1844 treaty that opened five new Chinese ports to American merchants. An overland route called the Old Spanish Trail allowed goods to be carried in both directions between California and Santa Fe. From there the Santa Fe Trail connected New Mexico with St. Louis, Missouri.

The need for trade increased as the American economy boomed. There had been a financial panic, and then a depression from 1837 to 1841, but now manufacturers were regaining their strength. Factories sprouted across the Northeast, producing textiles and household goods—tin and wood products, machine tools, furniture. Manufacturers with goods to sell needed markets, as did farmers with surplus crops. The building of canals and railroads in the 1830s and 1840s made trade easier. Railroads also meant that one day the vast territories of the West could be opened up to settlement and industry.

At the same time, the population of the United States was booming. Over 500,000 immigrants, mostly from Ireland and Germany, came to the United States in the 1830s. Nearly three times as many came in the 1840s. They helped build the canals and railroads, worked in factories, and settled farms on the frontier. They provided new markets for the goods produced by manufacturers. With the help of immigrants, the American population nearly doubled, from 12.9 million in 1830 to 23.2 million in 1850. Those who wanted to go west welcomed the gaining of new territory.

The slaveowners of the South also welcomed new territory. Cotton planting as it was practiced then tended to wear out the land, and the planters were forced to move west. Control of territory would also increase the political power of slaveowners in Congress. Southerners at that time were furiously defending slavery against the attacks of abolitionists who wanted to outlaw it and congressmen who wanted to limit its expansion. New Mexico and California were not suited to growing cotton, but Texas was. Southern politicians pushed for annexation of Texas to help strengthen their position.

Mexico, however, was determined to retain its northern provinces—both out of national pride and to prevent the further expansion of the United States. For similar reasons, Mexico refused to recognize Texas and even tried to reconquer it. Mexican troops twice invaded Texas in 1842; Texas responded by raiding a Mexican town.

The dispute over slavery and the fear that annexation would lead to war kept the United States from admitting Texas. But with a hostile neighbor, limited resources, and a large national debt, Texas needed a protector. Great Britain was eager to play that role, since an independent Texas would limit American expansion and act as an alternative trading partner. Britain helped arrange a cease-fire between Texas and Mexico in 1843, and considered mediating, with France, a more lasting peace treaty between the two countries.

Some Americans became alarmed at Britain's involvement. That fear was fueled by a rumor that Britain, which had abolished slavery in its own colonies, was planning to push for abolition in Texas. Like the theory that the British

This woodcut, titled "Discussing the Texas Question" shows Americans debating the proposed annexation of Texas as a state.

had designs on California, the story was probably untrue, but it helped the administration of President John Tyler fight for annexation.

On February 28, 1845, Congress approved a joint resolution inviting Texas to enter the Union. As expected, Mexico protested, and by the end of March it had cut off diplomatic relations. This step was serious, but it did not necessarily mean war. It took a series of events in the following year to make war inevitable. Not the least of these events was the inauguration that same March of President James K. Polk.

Polk had been elected the previous November on a platform that called for

American politics in the 1840s was high-spirited, as seen in this painting of election results being announced in a small town.

expansion into Texas and the Oregon territory. He was a serious, secretive man in his forties, unknown to most Americans, and had won only slightly more of the popular vote than his Whig opponent, Henry Clay. But he took his victory as a mandate for pursuing vigorous expansion across the continent.

Polk's strongest support was in the South, where people favored annexation of Texas and where Polk had once been governor of Tennessee. Polk also appealed to a more broad-based sentiment: the belief that the people of the United States, with their democratic government and free-market economy, were destined to spread all across the continent, and perhaps beyond. The Indians and Mexicans already living in the West were regarded either as obstacles or as barely civilized people who stood to benefit from America's superior institutions.

These expansionist views were expressed most strongly in journals controlled by Polk's Democratic party. In 1845 John L. O'Sullivan, editor of the *United States Magazine and Democratic Review*, coined the phrase that came to symbolize the notion: "manifest destiny." The inexpensive newspapers flourishing at the time—the "penny press"—quickly made the phrase a household word.

"Manifest destiny" meant many things to many people. Some came to see no limits to possible American expansion: into Canada, into Mexico, into South America, perhaps even back into Europe. Some felt that expansion should be peaceful; others were ready to consider war as a means of accomplishing it. The journal *The Harbinger* opposed war but felt that God might use war as a way "of extending the power and intelligence of advanced civilized nations over the whole face of the earth." Others, such as the Reverend Theodore Parker, felt that the noble goal of exporting "the Idea of America—that all men are born free and equal in rights"—required the United States to "first make real those ideas at home."

"Manifest destiny" did mean many things, but for Polk it meant one thing: expansion to the Pacific Ocean. That expansion would secure the Pacific ports for trade and open up the lands in between. The much vaguer notion of manifest destiny, as expressed in political speeches and in the popular press, was used by Polk to support his well-defined purpose.

Texas and Oregon were two steps toward that goal. On his last day in office, in March 1845, President Tyler had already sent a formal annexation proposal to Texas. President Polk now sent special agents to encourage Texans to accept the proposal. One of the inducements was that the United States would support Texas in its boundary dispute with Mexico.

The dispute was over which river constituted the southern boundary of Texas. Mexico claimed it was the Nueces River, as had been outlined on maps since the time of Spanish rule. Texas claimed that the southern and western boundary was the Rio Grande, about 150 miles south of the Nueces. Sam Houston had forced General Santa Anna to agree to that border after the Battle of San Jacinto, but Mexico had never considered the agreement to be binding.

In June 1845 Polk declared that Texas's claim would be upheld and that he would "not permit an invading enemy to occupy a foot of the soil East of the Rio Grande." At the end of June, General Zachary Taylor, stationed in Louisiana, received orders to move his troops to Corpus Christi, Texas, on the Nueces River. From there he was to wait for further instructions to advance to the Rio Grande. A Colonel Hitchcock in Taylor's army, knowing what the consequences of such a movement would be, wrote in his diary: "Violence leads to violence, and if this movement of ours does not lead to others and to bloodshed, I am much mistaken."

Polk was taking a great chance in moving toward war with Mexico, since many believed that the United States would soon be at war with Britain. The dispute with Britain had to do with the Oregon Territory: the land south of Alaska and north of California, from the Pacific Ocean to the continental divide. American expansionists claimed that the whole territory up to latitude 54° 40' (the southern tip of Alaska) belonged to the United States, while Britain insisted the United States had no title north of the Columbia River (which today marks the northern boundary of Oregon). Since 1818 Britain and the United States had jointly occupied the disputed land, but as clamor for a settlement increased on both sides, that compromise was no longer satisfactory.

Polk had suggested in the election that he would assert the U.S. claim all the way to 54° 40′, which became the subject of the expansionist slogan "Fifty-four Forty or Fight!" In reality, Polk was not prepared to go to war with Britain at the same time that war with Mexico seemed imminent. In the end, he agreed to a compromise extending the northern boundary of the United States along latitude 49° to the Pacific. That boundary was approved by Congress in 1846 and has remained the boundary to the present day.

While the Oregon dispute simmered and General Taylor's troops waited for orders in Texas, Polk made his first moves toward acquiring California. In June 1845 the navy in the Pacific made preparations to invade California if war came with Mexico. An expedition led by army captain John Frémont set out to explore in the region, where it could also lend military support if needed. In October the American consul at Monterey was told to take advantage of any native unrest in hope of convincing Californians to revolt against Mexico. That same fall, Frémont's report of an earlier journey gave Americans their first detailed information about California.

Polk finally made his one determined effort to settle the Texas question and

John C. Frémont's account of his explorations in California fueled American interest in acquiring Mexico's northern territories.

buy California without war. In November 1845 he commissioned John Slidell as minister to the Mexican government of José Herrera.

Slidell was to use America's financial claims against Mexico as a bargaining tool. The claims, which included damage to American property during Mexico's civil wars, amounted to some $4 million. The United States would assume all claims in exchange for recognition of the Rio Grande as its southern boundary. Slidell was also to offer various amounts for New Mexico and California.

THE TRIBUNE.

From our Extra of Yesterday Morning.

BY ELECTRIC TELEGRAPH!

CABINET AT WASHINGTON CONVENED
ON SUNDAY MORNING.

50,000 VOLUNTEERS CALLED FOR!

$10,000,000 TO BE RAISED!

Additional and important particulars of War with Mexico!!!

REINFORCEMENT OF PT. ISABEL BY CREWS
OF U. S. VESSELS FLIRT AND LAWRENCE!!

No Mexicans between Pt. Isabel & Gen. Taylor.

Gen. GAINES again in the Field.

The New-York Daily Tribune announces the out-break of the Mexican War and a call for volunteers. Many volunteers were needed to supplement the tiny U.S. regular army.

With anger against the United States still running high in Mexico, and with many political enemies waiting for a chance to unseat him, President Herrera did not dare to negotiate with Slidell. Even so, the story spread that he was betraying Mexico to the Americans. General Mariano Paredes led a revolt and, on January 2, became president.

On January 13, 1846, the day after word came to Washington of the failure of Slidell's mission, President Polk made his move. He ordered General Taylor to leave the Nueces River and advance to the Rio Grande. Taylor did so. His army marched across the barren region; the Mexicans who lived on the disputed side of the Rio Grande fled. On March 28 Taylor's army arrived. They aimed their cannons at the Mexican city of Matamoros on the other side of the river, and waited.

President Polk was ready to order Taylor into war. According to his diary, he told his cabinet on May 9 that in his opinion there was "ample cause" for war, and that it was impossible for him to remain silent any longer. He and his cabinet agreed, however, that first the Mexicans would have to attack Taylor. Unless the Mexicans attacked, any U.S. attack would be seen as unjust and unnecessary. Polk was waiting for the incident that would make war acceptable.

That very evening, Polk received a dispatch from General Taylor. Taylor reported that on April 25 a Mexican force had crossed the Rio Grande and attacked an American patrol, killing or wounding sixteen. "Hostilities," Taylor stated, "may now be considered as commenced."

On May 11 Polk sent a message to Congress. "The cup of forbearance had been exhausted even before the recent information," he stated. "But now, after reiterated menaces, Mexico has passed the boundary of the United States, has invaded our territory and shed American blood upon the American soil."

It was highly disputable, of course, that the left bank of the Rio Grande was

American soil. Historically, it had belonged to Mexico. It was clear to many that the purpose of the war was to acquire California and New Mexico, which then included Arizona. Polk denied privately that such was his purpose, but he refused to state it in an official letter. Taylor's subordinate Colonel Hitchcock wrote: "It looks as if the government sent a small force on purpose to bring on a war, so as to have a pretext for taking California and as much of this country as it chooses."

Despite the opposition of some members, Congress declared war. In fact, however, it could only ratify a war that was already being fought. On May 9, even as word came to Polk of the initial skirmish, cannons were firing near the Rio Grande and Taylor's army battled fiercely with a force three times its size. The Mexican War had begun.

3

THE WAR

Taylor's army worked night and day building forts on the Rio Grande after their first skirmish with the Mexicans. On May 7 about 2,000 soldiers left the fort at the river's mouth, weary from raising walls and barricades. They marched back toward the other fort at Matamoros with a huge wagon train of supplies. On May 8, at about three in the afternoon, at a watering hole called Palo Alto, they met the enemy.

General Mariano Arista had led some 6,000 Mexicans across the Rio Grande to drive out the invaders. The Americans were outnumbered and weighed down by their wagon train. But the battle was decided by the quality of artillery. The Mexican cannons were weak and inaccurate, while the American weapons were deadly. After an hour, the punish-

Americans reacted with excitement to news of the war with Mexico, as shown in this painting. Many men rushed off to join the volunteers raised for the fighting, but others protested against a war they called unjust.

ing bombardment routed the Mexicans. The Americans had suffered 55 casualties, the Mexicans over 200.

General Arista's troops retreated to a brush-covered ravine called the Resaca de la Palma. There they waited for the pursuing Americans. On the afternoon of May 9, in fierce hand-to-hand fighting, the Mexicans were again scattered by Taylor's men. The Americans suffered 150 casualties, while 1,200 Mexicans were killed or wounded.

This time Arista's soldiers fled back across the Rio Grande to the fortified town of Matamoros. Taylor prepared to attack, but Arista had no intention of facing him. Arista stalled for time by discussing truce terms while he quietly evacuated his troops. On May 18 Taylor's men crossed the river into Matamoros only to find it undefended. They occupied it, and for the first time raised the American flag over a Mexican town.

News of the victories at Palo Alto and Resaca de la Palma soon reached the United States. Newspaper accounts

General Zachary Taylor, on horseback, directs his troops at the Battle of Palo Alto on May 8, 1846.

made Taylor a national hero. Nicknamed "Old Rough and Ready" for his blunt manner and plain habits, Taylor began to be talked about as a possible candidate for the White House.

But Taylor and his soldiers could not claim all the credit. Their victories owed something to the weaknesses of the Mexican army. The Mexican soldiers outnumbered the Americans, but they were often poorly disciplined and poorly led. Too many officers had gotten their commissions through family connections, not through their ability. Mexico had few factories to make weap-

ons. Its artillery was hopelessly outdated. Its cavalry was dashing, but easily cut down by American cannon and sharpshooters.

Perhaps most fatally, Mexico's leaders suffered from severe overconfidence. They had believed that the United States would never dare go to war, and that if it did, it would soon be defeated. When Mexico did lose in battle, its leaders were all too ready to blame one another. Unstable, nearly bankrupt, Mexico was in a poor position to fight and win a war.

On the other hand, the United States

had weaknesses of its own. Its leaders, too, fought among themselves—the president with his generals, Democrats with Whigs. Americans suffered from their own overconfidence, expecting the war to be shorter and less costly than it was. Taylor's army was poorly supplied and unfamiliar with the terrain. Most American soldiers looked down at Mexicans, expecting them to be lazy and cowardly. They were often painfully surprised when the Mexicans fought back.

With Taylor camped at Matamoros, Polk and his advisers planned strategy for the war. Taylor's army would march deeper into northern Mexico. Another force, the Army of the West, had set out before to conquer New Mexico and California. The navy would help by attacking California and blockading the enemy's ports on the Gulf of Mexico, keeping supplies from going in or out. With no effective navy of its own, Mexico could do little to resist the blockade.

Polk hoped that these strategies alone would quickly persuade Mexico to make peace. He did not yet realize that Mexico would keep fighting, only giving up when its capital was in enemy hands.

Taylor's first objective was the northern city of Monterrey. Nestled in the foothills of the Sierra Madre, Monterrey

Taylor's victory at Palo Alto was followed by another at Resaca de la Palma on May 9, 1846.

VOLUNTEERS!

Men of the Granite State!

Men of Old Rockingham!! the

strawberry-bed of patriotism, renowned for bravery and devotion to Country, rally at this call. Santa Anna, reeking with the generous confidence and magnanimity of your countrymen, is in arms, eager to plunge his traitor-dagger in their bosoms. To arms, then, and rush to the standard of the fearless and gallant CUSHING—put to the blush the dastardly meanness and rank toryism of Massachusetts. Let the half civilized Mexicans hear the crack of the unerring New Hampshire rifleman, and illustrate on the plains of San Luis Potosi, the fierce, determined, and undaunted bravery that has always characterized her sons.

Col. THEODORE F. ROWE, at No. 81 Daniel-street, is authorized and will enlist men this week for the Massachusetts Regiment of Volunteers. The compensation is $10 per month---$30 in advance. Congress will grant a handsome bounty in money and ONE HUNDRED AND SIXTY ACRES OF LAND.

Portsmouth, Feb. 2, 1847.

Although this poster calls for volunteers from New Hampshire, the Mexican War was unpopular with many New Englanders, who saw it as a move to grab new slave territory for the South.

guarded a vital mountain pass leading to Mexico's interior. Mexican troops assembled there. As they fortified the walls of rock that protected the city, Taylor advanced in their direction.

Taylor's advance was slowed down by several obstacles. One was his feud with President Polk. The Democrat Polk was convinced that Taylor, a Whig, was scheming to be the country's next president. This belief only grew stronger as Taylor's fame spread. At the same time, Taylor sent frequent complaints to Washington—about bad planning, lack of supplies, and the unsatisfactory volunteers he was being sent.

Taylor had reason to complain about the volunteers. In 1836 the United States had a standing army of only about 7,500 men. About a third of these were foreign-born, with little cause for loyalty. Congress had ordered the states to enlist 50,000 volunteers to supplement the regular army. But many of these men came with little equipment and less discipline. They were all too ready to go home at the end of their terms of service—usually a year, sometimes as little as three months. Not surprisingly, quarrels and even riots became common between the regular troops and the volunteers.

Another obstacle was disease. Living without enough shelter, in unsanitary camp conditions, the soldiers found disease to be more deadly than the Mexicans were. As the army marched up the Rio Grande toward Monterrey, hundreds died of dysentery and other diseases. Their suffering increased when they camped for six weeks in the hot and humid town of Camargo. One soldier called the town a "Yawning Graveyard."

Taylor's 7,000 men began to arrive on the outskirts of Monterrey on September 19. Inside the stone city, roughly the same number of Mexican soldiers were completing their fortifications. Monterrey was well stocked with supplies and protected by forts, barricades, and natural heights. It seemed impossible to capture.

American troops fight their way into Monterrey. The heavily-fortified city fell on September 23, 1846.

The Americans tried on September 20. For the next three days Taylor's subordinate, General William Jenkins Worth, led two thousand men on a flanking movement west of the city and fought for control of two fortified hills. At the same time, Taylor attacked from the east, bombarding and charging the city. A heavy rain fell during much of the battle. Casualties ran high—some 500 Americans were killed or wounded. American soldiers finally broke into the city, but the Mexicans resisted, fighting in the streets and from house to house.

Finally, Taylor found his troops weary and short of supplies. He was prepared to negotiate. On September 24 the Mexicans surrendered Monterrey, but their army was allowed to retreat safely and a temporary armistice was signed.

Although Taylor considered this the best deal he could make, President Polk was outraged. He believed Taylor's action would prolong the war. "He had the enemy in his grasp and should have taken them prisoner," wrote Polk. The president decided that a new commanding general and a new strategy were needed.

Polk was thinking as a practical politician. If he did not end the war soon,

Henry David Thoreau. His one-man protest against the Mexican War influenced Mahatma Gandhi, Dr. Martin Luther King, Jr., and many others.

his party would lose popularity. At first, the war had been popular in much of the United States. Southern states had no trouble raising volunteers. Democratic newspapers supported Polk. Poets and playwrights made the war seem romantic. Readers of the popular newspapers enjoyed hearing about battles, as reported by the first American "war correspondents." The Mexican War was also one of the first wars ever to be photographed, though few of the daguerreotypes taken have survived.

But many Americans were against the war. These included newspaper editor Horace Greeley and abolitionists like William Lloyd Garrison—people who wanted an end to slavery. Groups of workingmen in the Northeast said that the war was simply an effort to gain new lands for slaveowners. The American Peace Society in Boston called the war unprovoked aggression—a case of one power, the United States, starting a fight with another. The Reverend Theodore Parker urged people not to volunteer to fight or make weapons.

Philosopher Henry David Thoreau made a protest in Massachusetts that had far-reaching effects. In 1846 he spent a night in jail for refusing to pay a tax supporting the war. His action did not stop the war, but all over the world it became an example to people struggling for justice (see sidebar).

In Congress, most Whigs opposed the war. Voters increased their numbers in the election of November 1846, which brought critics of the war, like Illinois representative Abraham Lincoln, into Congress. But their criticism was mostly talk. Since they did not want to seem disloyal, most of them voted for measures to fund the war. Only a few followed the example of Joshua Giddings of Ohio, who voted against all measures that would aid in "the murder of Mexicans upon their own soil, or in robbing them of their country."

The army and navy pressed forward while Congress debated. Colonel Stephen Kearny was leading 1,500 men from Fort Leavenworth, Kansas, along the Santa Fe Trail to New Mexico, as Taylor marched toward Monterrey. On August 18, 1846, after a march of 900 miles, Kearny's men occupied Santa Fe without firing a shot. The Mexican gov-

CIVIL DISOBEDIENCE

Henry David Thoreau had not paid his Massachusetts poll tax for several years when the Concord tax collector stopped him in the street. The month was July 1846, war was raging in Mexico, and the government needed money. The twenty-nine-year-old philosopher refused to pay. He was put in jail.

Thoreau was not in jail for long. Against his will, someone—a friend or family member—paid the back taxes for him. He was freed the next morning. That might have been the end of the story, except that the people of Concord were curious about Thoreau's actions. In January 1848, days before a peace treaty was signed in Mexico, Thoreau explained his actions in a lecture at the Concord Lyceum.

"Witness the present Mexican war, the work of comparatively a few individuals using the standing government as their tool. . . . How does it become a man to behave toward this American government to-day? I answer that he cannot without disgrace be associated with it."

"Must the citizen ever for a moment, or in the least degree, resign his conscience to the legislator? Why has every man a conscience, then?"

"If [the machine of government] is of such a nature that it requires you to be the agent of injustice to another, then, I say, break the law. Let your life be a counter friction to stop the machine."

Thoreau urged people who were opposed to slavery and the war to do something about it. Refusing to pay taxes might result in jail, but it was a duty. If enough people peacefully resisted, the government would be forced to surrender.

Thoreau's lecture, later titled "Civil Disobedience," was published in essay form in 1849. Ignored at the time, it has since become famous throughout the world.

The essay's new life began about 1900, when India was under oppressive British rule. An Indian law student named Mohandas Gandhi came across Thoreau's "Civil Disobedience" and saw it as a tool for change. In South Africa as well as India, Gandhi applied Thoreau's ideas. Thousands of "civil resisters" broke the law peacefully and willingly went to jail. Faced with a people who refused to cooperate, the government had to change. In 1947, after some thirty years of struggle, India won its independence.

Gandhi was not the only one to apply Thoreau's techniques. Under Nazi occupation during World War II, Thoreau was a hero to the people of Denmark as they resisted the Germans. In the United States, protestors against the draft and laborers on strike have read and used "Civil Disobedience." In the 1950s and 1960s, the successful movement of American blacks against segregation laws in the South was partly shaped by the fact that Martin Luther King, Jr., had read Thoreau in college.

Thoreau's night in jail did not affect the course of the Mexican War. But what he called the action of "one honest man" has affected the course of history.

Colonel Stephen Kearny and his small force marched 1,800 miles, from Kansas to Santa Fe.

Commodore John Sloat's ships fire a salute as U.S. Marines raise the American flag over Monterey, California, on July 7, 1846.

ernor had already evacuated his army because he favored American rule.

At first, California seemed to fall as easily as New Mexico. Captain John C. Frémont, the explorer who had been in the area since the previous year, led a revolt in Sonoma in July 1846. With no support from the rest of the province, they declared California an independent republic on July 4. The leaders of the so-called republic raised a "Bear Flag" that was replaced a few days later with the American flag.

Around the same time, the navy under Commodore John Sloat seized the vital ports of Monterey and San Francisco. The ailing Sloat was replaced by Robert Stockton. Stockton captured the enemy stronghold of Los Angeles without opposition on August 12. For the moment, it appeared that both California and New Mexico were safely in American hands.

The appearance was deceptive. The Californians revolted and succeeded in taking back Los Angeles on September 22. In the following months, the Mexicans secured their hold on most of the towns in California's interior. Kearny and 150 men journeyed from New Mexico to reinforce Stockton, but had to fight through enemy lines to reach him. Not until January 10, 1847, did Stockton's forces again take possession of Los Angeles.

The people of New Mexico proved almost as hard to conquer. Although Santa Fe appeared to be at peace, in December a plot to overthrow the Americans was discovered. Even as the occu-

This fanciful lithograph depicts U.S. dragoons—infantry mounted on horseback—in action in Mexico.

pation force cracked down, the rebellion spread across the province. It was not crushed until February. The Mexican army may have been easy to defeat, but the Mexican people were not. The rebellion was not crushed until February.

American soldiers won victories in New Mexico and California. Since those battles were far away from the center of Mexico, however, they were not likely to convince the government to seek terms of peace. A small force led by Alexander Doniphan, one of Kearny's volunteers, captured the city of Chihuahua in March 1847. But that too was far away. Even General Taylor, as he ad-

vanced through northern Mexico, had no immediate hope of striking a crushing blow. A new strategy was needed.

President Polk decided on an ancient invasion route—the route Hernán Cortés and his conquistadors had followed when they overthrew the Aztec empire. The route led from the port of Veracruz on the Gulf of Mexico, through the mountains, to the gates of Mexico City. On November 22, 1846, General Winfield Scott was assigned to lead the campaign. Polk did not like Scott much more than he liked Taylor. Like Taylor, Scott was an outspoken Whig who had been named as a possible presidential candidate. Scott was vain and domi-

Mexican "guerrilleros" (guerrilla fighters) like the ones pictured harassed American troops in the rugged Mexican countryside.

neering—nicknamed "Old Fuss and Feathers" by his men. But as a veteran leader, and as general-in-chief of the army since 1841, he was the man for the job.

To accomplish his mission, Scott was forced to take troops from General Taylor in January 1847. That left Taylor with fewer than 5,000 men to meet a force of nearly 20,000 Mexicans marching toward them across the desert. In a mountain pass near a ranch called Buena Vista, the Americans fought off the Mexicans for two days, February 22 and 23. Although both sides suffered heavy losses, the Mexicans took the worst of it and finally withdrew. This American victory, of little importance to the outcome of the war, did seal Taylor's status as a popular hero.

The Battle of Buena Vista was also important for the man who led the Mexicans. That man was General Santa Anna, the former dictator who had wiped out the Texans at the Alamo eleven years earlier. Many Mexicans hated Santa Anna, but he was the best officer they had. They welcomed him back as commander and president.

Ironically, it was President Polk who made it possible for Santa Anna to return. The general had been living in exile in Cuba during one of the periods when the Mexicans had forced him out. He led Polk to believe that if he was restored to power, he would help the United States end the war. Polk ordered the navy to allow Santa Anna to pass through the blockade and return home. But within weeks, Santa Anna was rais-

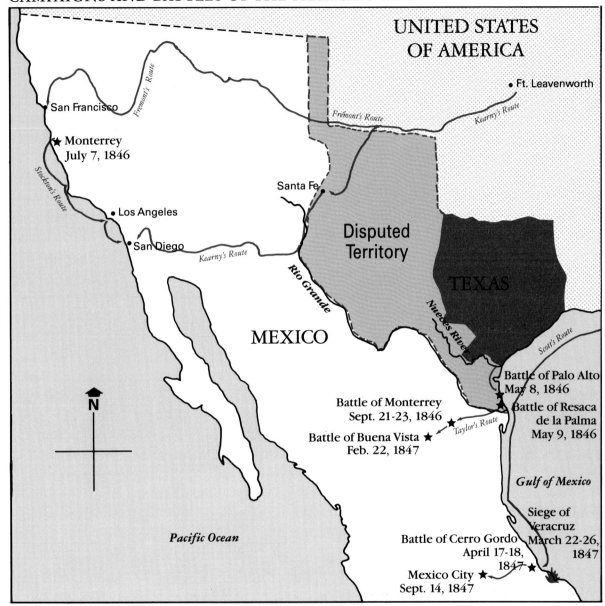

ing an enormous army to drive out the Americans.

For the moment, however, Santa Anna's army was recovering from its defeat at Buena Vista. The Mexican army retreated back toward the capital while General Scott and his fleet sailed along the coast to the vicinity of Veracruz. On March 9, 1847, Scott launched the largest amphibious assault ever attempted by American troops, attacking with both land and sea forces. Ten thousand soldiers waded from surf boats onto the beach as naval gunfire provided cover. The Mexicans did not resist. That was their first step toward defeat.

4

CONQUEST

The port city of Veracruz was walled, fortified, and guarded by 4,000 troops. Rather than trying a direct assault, General Scott laid siege to Veracruz. His troops sealed off the city in a line seven miles long so that the citizens of Veracruz could neither escape nor receive help. On March 22, 1847, Scott called for the city's surrender. When he was refused, he ordered the bombardment to begin.

The bombardment lasted two days. Thousands of shells rained into the city, smashing buildings, starting fires, and killing hundreds of people. Most of the dead and wounded were not soldiers but women and children. Scott refused to allow such noncombatants to leave, since their presence would help force the Mexicans to surrender. On March 29 Scott's forces marched into the city and raised the American flag.

The young cadets of the Mexican Military Academy, one of whom is pictured here—fought to the death defending Chapultepec Castle from the attacking Americans.

Engineers trained at the U.S. Military Academy at West Point had helped plan the siege. Junior officers like Lieutenant P.G.T. Beauregard placed artillery, scouted territory, and advised on tactics. Other West Point-trained officers in Mexico included Ulysses S. Grant, Robert E. Lee, George McClellan, and Thomas Jackson, later to win fame as "Stonewall" Jackson. Their efficiency and courage made West Point famous, at a time when Congress had been talking about closing the academy. What no one could have foreseen was that the same officers who earned such high praise would one day use their training to ravage each other's armies in the American Civil War.

The Americans were now about 200 miles from Mexico City. Before them lay the route of conquest Cortés had taken in 1521. Many of the soldiers were inspired by a romantic idea of what Cortés had done. They had read about it in a popular book, William Prescott's *History of the Conquest of Mexico*. But

Cannon aboard U.S. Navy ships pound Veracruz prior to the landing of 10,000 soldiers.

those who were veterans knew that more than romance lay ahead: pain, fear, and almost impossible odds. Back home, many doubted that the small army had a chance at victory. President Polk himself thought little of Scott's abilities, and Scott felt a "total want of support or sympathy on the part of the War Department."

Santa Anna soon learned of the fall of Veracruz and returned to Mexico City to raise more funds and more troops. He had wasted time fighting Taylor in the north when the war had been taken to the center of Mexico. Santa Anna had been driven from office once before for losing to the Americans—in Texas in 1836. The same thing would happen if he failed now.

On April 8 Scott's army began to move out of Veracruz. They took the National Highway into the mountains, where they would be safe from the yellow fever that plagued the lowlands in the summer months. Just below the pass of Cerro Gordo, they found Santa Anna's army blocking the highway in a line two miles long, their cannons aimed directly at the American column.

Santa Anna thought his army's position was impassable, but the Americans proved otherwise. On April 18 they attacked the Mexican right. Santa Anna's troops repelled the attack, only to find that it was a diversion. The bulk of Scott's troops moved around the Mexican left and attacked from the rear. In the confusion, the Mexican line fell apart. Three thousand Mexicans were taken prisoner; the rest fled.

By May the Americans had taken three towns with little opposition. They rested in the city of Puebla, about 75 miles from Mexico City. The capital was in an uproar. Santa Anna arrested critics and called the public to even greater sacrifices. He drafted civilians to help build defenses and swelled the number of troops to over 25,000.

Scott's army, however, was dwindling. Seven regiments of volunteers went home when their twelve-month terms of enlistment were over. Desertion increased as well, as soldiers grew weary of discipline, hard labor, and death. By war's end, 9,000 Americans had deserted their regiments throughout Mexico. Disease further cut into Scott's ranks, while the people of Puebla threatened to revolt against his troops.

By early August reinforcements had arrived. Scott rebuilt his army to a force of 14,000. They left Puebla on the last leg of their journey on August 7. From

Mexican forces surrender to General Winfield Scott as the American flag is raised over Veracruz on March 29, 1847.

a mountain crest they caught the first glimpse of Mexico City, shining among the vast marshes far below. The view was beautiful, but also sobering. Mexico City was walled and surrounded by fortresses. It could only be entered by causeways, roads built across the wetlands. Troops and artillery guarded every approach.

The Mexican defense was weakest south and west of the city. That was the route General Scott chose to take. Santa Anna quickly shifted troops to that area, but Scott kept him off balance. At Contreras on August 20, a Mexican force fired at what it thought was the main body of the Americans. In fact, most of the invading army had slipped silently to the rear. They routed the startled Mexicans in 17 minutes.

That was to be the last easy battle. As they drew near to the capital, the Americans were made to pay dearly for every victory. At the Churubusco River, 3 miles from Mexico City, 4,000 Mexicans were killed or wounded defending a bridge and a fortified convent. The Americans won, but suffered about 1,000 casualties.

The Americans also received a surprise. Among those they had been fighting were two companies of American deserters. Most of these deserters, known as the "San Patricios," were foreign-born men, Irish or German. They had been discriminated against in camp and had lost their loyalty to the United States. As Roman Catholics, they felt a kinship with the Mexicans. The Americans showed no mercy to the captured

deserters in the trials that followed. Fifty-nine were hanged, two were shot, and seven were punished by whipping and branding.

Santa Anna, having been pushed back to Mexico City, used a trick that other Mexican generals had found handy—stalling for time by suing for peace. He convinced General Scott to agree to stop fighting while both sides tried to reach a settlement. Meanwhile, he prepared for the final defense of the capital. When the talks ended without success, Scott faced the prospect of fierce Mexican resistance.

Two fortified positions guarded the southwestern entrance to the capital. One was a foundry for making cannon, called Molino del Rey; the other was a castle and military school, called Chapultepec. On September 8 Scott ordered his troops to capture Molino del Rey. They did, but the battle was costly and, unknown to Scott, all but useless. Only a few cannon were found in the buildings.

Chapultepec, on the other hand, was both difficult and vital to capture. Its guns were aimed at the gates that the Americans would have to use to enter the city. On September 12 American artillery began pounding Chapultepec. The infantry stormed the castle the next day. Using ladders, the Americans climbed the walls and battled the Mexicans hand to hand. The young cadets of the military school were among the bravest defenders. Many of them fought to the death rather than surrender. They are still remembered in Mexican history as *Los Niños Héroes*—the boy heroes.

The story of the war was nearly finished. The Americans swept on past the castle to the gates of Mexico City. The next morning at daybreak, an unarmed Mexican carried the white flag of truce from the citadel that guarded the city. Santa Anna had evacuated the army during the night, heading north to a suburb called Guadalupe Hidalgo. Mexico City had fallen to the Americans.

Santa Anna led one last attack on the Americans stationed at Puebla, which was easily fought off. He was blamed for the country's defeat and was banished from Mexico. It fell to his successor, President Pedro Anaya, to make peace with the United States.

President Polk was apparently hoping to humble the Mexican government. On October 6 he ordered peace commissioner Nicholas Trist to return home; the Mexicans would have to go to Washington to ask for terms. But Trist was already preparing to negotiate with Mexico's new president. Trist disobeyed orders and stayed.

Polk was furious, but he could not find fault with the treaty that Trist negotiated. It was signed in Guadalupe Hidalgo on February 2, 1848, and it gave the Americans everything they had gone to war for. Mexico gave up its claim to Texas and accepted the Rio Grande boundary. The rest of Mexico's Far North, including California, was sold to the United States. These lands, called the Mexican Cession, included what is today California, Nevada, and

General Winfield Scott reviews his troops. Scott's entry into Mexico City marked the end of the war.

Utah, with parts of New Mexico, Arizona, Wyoming, and Colorado.

The United States paid Mexico $15 million for the land, and also took on $3 million in unpaid claims of American citizens against Mexico. The total price was cheaper than anything the United States could have negotiated peacefully—except for the thousands killed and wounded on both sides.

The rights of Mexicans living in what was now the American Southwest were protected by the terms of the treaty. Mexicans who chose to remain were granted "all the rights of citizens of the

UNITED STATES ACQUISITIONS FROM MEXICO

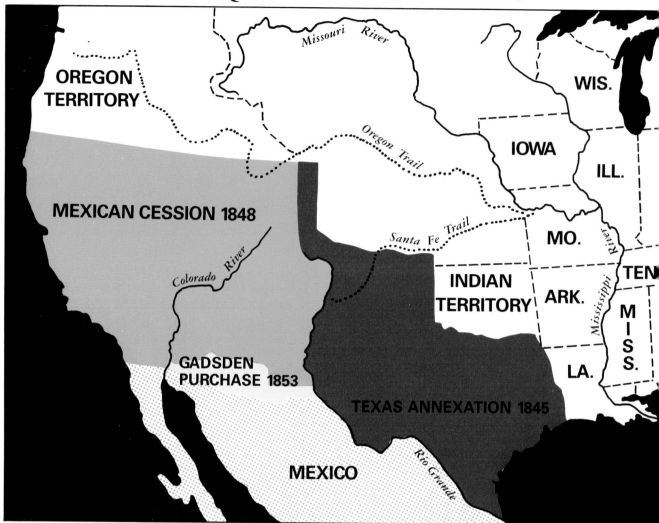

United States," including religious, property, and political rights. They were soon to discover how easily these rights could be violated.

Some Americans insisted that the United States could get still more land, and called for the conquest of all of Mexico. Congress decided otherwise. The U.S. Senate ratified the Treaty of Guadalupe Hidalgo on March 10. The Mexican Congress did the same on March 25. On June 12 the conquerors marched out of Mexico City. By the end of July, the last American troops had left the country.

About two years had passed since the first American regiment marched into Mexico. Over 13,000 Americans had died, mostly of disease. On the Mexican side, thousands more died in battle than did Americans. Civilians suffered too, either in bombardments such as those at Veracruz, or by the crimes of the American occupation troops—despite orders from Washington to be lenient. Some of General Taylor's regiments in particular were notorious for murdering, robbing, and raping.

American veterans, returning home, brought pieces of the culture to the United States. Mustaches became popular. So did little cigars wrapped in paper—*cigarritos*, or cigarettes. Buena Vista and Palo Alto became popular names for new towns. As the new territories were settled, Spanish words like *lasso*, *corral*, and *patio* entered the English language. The word *vaquero*, meaning cowboy, was turned into "buckaroo."

Veterans faced economic problems. They had won bounties of land for their service but were more often in need of hard cash. Many of them sold their 160 acres to speculators for less than $50. Some soldiers, however, did quite well. In 1848 General Taylor was elected to the White House, just as Polk had feared. General Scott ran for the same job in 1852, but was defeated by Franklin Pierce. However, he remained in the U.S. Army until he retired in 1861. Today, many consider him the greatest American commander of the first half of the nineteenth century.

A new army now began to cross into the territories obtained through war—an army not of soldiers but of prospectors, settlers, and businessmen. In January 1848, even before the treaty with Mexico was signed, gold was discovered at John Sutter's mill in California. The news spread quickly, and by 1849

A popular figure because of his Mexican War victories, Zachary Taylor, "Old Rough and Ready," was elected president on the Whig ticket in 1848.

Americans from every part of the country raced to the west coast to seek their fortune. Some found gold; most didn't. But thanks to these "forty-niners," California grew. The gold that the early Spanish explorers had looked for in the Far North had finally been found—but too late to benefit Mexico. The profits went to American citizens.

The United States had still not acquired all the land it wanted from Mexico. In 1853 an agreement called the Gadsden Purchase set the southern boundaries of Arizona and New Mexico as we know them today. American mining interests wanted the mineral wealth

In 1849, a year after the Mexican War ended, gold was discovered in California. Thousands of "forty-niners" flocked to the gold fields.

of the Mesilla Valley, which was owned by Mexico. The government wanted to build a railroad through the valley to by-pass the Rocky Mountains. James Gadsden, the American foreign minister, convinced Mexico to sell the land for $10 million. The Mexican president at that time was once again Santa Anna. He was again sent into exile for helping the United States take Mexico's land.

Railroad owners bought vast tracts of land in the new territories, as did mining companies, land speculators, and cattlemen. Soon they were making great profits. The Mexican residents of the American Southwest enjoyed little of the new wealth. The peace treaty had granted these 80,000 people the rights of American citizens, but in the decades that followed, they were gradually stripped of their land.

Often Mexican residents lost their land through legal means. Mexican-Americans had to prove they owned their land with papers they did not have. Even if they won in court, they sometimes had to sell their land to pay their lawyers. Racial prejudice, violence, drought, high property taxes, and economic failure forced many other Mexican-Americans from their lands. By 1900 the Mexican-Americans of the Southwest were largely a landless people.

The ranks of Mexican-Americans, who came to be known as Chicanos in the 1960s, increased with immigration from Mexico beginning at the turn of the twentieth century. They worked on railroads, in mines, and on large farms. They were regarded as cheap labor and were paid lower wages than white

A wagon train of settlers pushes westward. The decades following the Mexican War saw manifest destiny fulfilled as farms, towns, cities, and railroads sprang up from the Mississippi River to the Pacific Ocean.

workers. Migration to the cities did not improve the lot of most Chicanos. Only in the twentieth century have Chicanos begun to better their conditions and defend their rights through labor unions and other forms of group action.

Native Americans in the Southwest were also forced off their land when the United States took over. Because Mexican rule had been weak, Native American peoples like the Navajo and the Apache had managed to keep a strong hold in the region. The United States government, however, forced them to submit to its authority. In the 1860s in New Mexico, men like Kit Carson were ordered to capture and kill Apaches and Navajos, destroy their food, and take their livestock. After 1868 the number of Navajos was half what it had been in 1863. The survivors who made peace were moved from their ancient lands to reservations.

For Native Americans and Mexican-Americans, the American conquest of the Southwest was hardly a victory. But many English-speaking Americans were proud that their country now stretched from the Atlantic to the Pacific. There were still critics of the war who claimed that the victory was unjust. But others claimed that the United

This lithograph, titled "Through to the Pacific," celebrates the Transcontinental Railroad. Completed in 1869, the railroad linked the East and Midwest with the west coast.

States had fulfilled its "manifest destiny" to expand across the continent. If so, America's destiny was also division, and war.

Immediately following the Mexican War, division arose over slavery. Many Americans, mostly in the North, did not want slavery to spread into the new territories. Southerners felt it had to, or else representatives of free states would outnumber them in Congress. The battle lines were drawn in 1846, when a Pennsylvania congressman named David Wilmot tried to make slavery illegal in any territories that might be acquired in the Mexican War. The Wilmot Proviso did not pass, but it set the terms of the long debate that followed.

Peace was made briefly with the Compromise of 1850. In five separate acts of legislation, North and South both made concessions. California was admitted as a free state, while slavery was allowed in the Utah and New Mexico territories.

The compromise did not last. In 1854, those who wanted to keep slavery from expanding formed the Republican Party. Southerners threatened to split away from the Union if a Republican won the White House. In November 1860, Republican Abraham Lincoln was elected. On December 20, South Carolina became the first state to secede from the United States.

Other Southern states soon followed. They formed a separate government, the Confederate States of Amer-

THE HERCULES OF THE UNION,
SLAYING THE GREAT DRAGON OF SECESSION.

Winfield Scott commanded the U.S. Army when the Civil War broke out, but he retired to West Point in the war's first year. This cartoon depicts Scott as the "Hercules of the Union." Many of the young officers he led in Mexico became Confederate generals.

ica. On April 12, 1861, the first shot of the American Civil War was fired on Fort Sumter, South Carolina. The Confederate general who gave the order to fire was P.G.T. Beauregard, who had helped to capture Mexico City. The Union commander he was firing at was Major Robert Anderson, who had served with him. Before long, nearly every officer who fought in the Mexican War chose one side or the other.

AFTERWORD

NEIGHBORS

The capture of Mexico City in 1847 was a stunning American victory. It brought the United States vast new territories. But it also raised problems.

One was a moral problem. The United States had fought what many, then and now, have considered an unjust war—a war of aggression. Those who believe that nations should follow rules of justice must take that issue seriously. Another problem was practical as well as moral. Would the new territories be slave or free? Americans were not ready to decide. This disagreement led the nation into the Civil War.

Perhaps the most lasting issue raised by the Mexican War is in the area of foreign relations. The war marked a new readiness on the part of the United States to send its armed forces abroad. Nowhere has that been clearer than in Latin America, where the capture of Mexico City was viewed with anger and fear.

Since the Mexican War, the United States has intervened in many parts of

San Antonio, Texas, home of the Alamo, as it looks today.

Latin America for many different reasons. In the 1850s, the United States sent troops to Argentina, Nicaragua, and Uruguay. The United States intervened 13 times in Panama between 1850 and 1900, and, in the early twentieth century, used its influence to build the Panama Canal. In the 1960s the United States supported an invasion of Cuba by exiled opponents of the Cuban government and sent troops to the Dominican Republic in response to an attempted revolution. In the 1980s American military advisers helped train local forces in El Salvador. U.S. troops invaded the island nation of Grenada in 1983.

The United States has used military force in Latin America for many reasons. One reason has been to enforce the Monroe Doctrine—to limit the influence of other foreign powers in the Western Hemisphere. In the mid-1800s, the rivals to be countered were Britain and France. Since 1959, when a Communist government took power in Cuba, the stated enemy has been the Soviet Union and its allies.

Another reason has been to protect

the economic interests of the United States. Since the nineteenth century, American businesses have counted on Latin America for markets, raw materials, and transportation routes. American companies like Texaco, Goodyear, and Chase Bank were all doing business in Cuba before 1959. Protection of these interests has often gone hand in hand with enforcement of the Monroe Doctrine. The United States opposed Fidel Castro in Cuba because of the ties he formed with the Soviet Union. But they also opposed him because he took over the assets of American companies.

Whatever the reasons, the crucial spots on the map where the United States intervenes often remain the same. In 1854, a United States warship bombarded and destroyed Greytown, a city in Nicaragua that was under British control. In the 1980s the United States has helped rebels trying to overthrow the Nicaraguan government, on the grounds that Nicaragua is under Soviet control.

Intervention may bring gratitude from the countries where the United States intervenes. But often it brings anger and distrust that may take years to overcome. The history of American relations with Mexico from the fall of Mexico City to the present is a case in point.

Less than twenty years after they went to war, the United States and Mexico became allies. In the early 1860s France invaded and occupied Mexico. The French placed a foreign emperor in power—Archduke Maximilian of Austria. Mexicans took up arms to drive him out.

The United States also wanted to drive Maximilian out. The French occupation clearly violated the Monroe Doctrine. But until 1865 the United States was caught up in its own civil war. Afterward, the United States pressured France to withdraw its troops. Mexican rebels were allowed to buy guns and ammunition in California. In 1867 the French were expelled. The interests of the United States and Mexico had coincided for perhaps the first time.

In the decades that followed, relations between the United States and Mexico grew friendly. The friendship was based on the alliance between the Mexican government and American business. President Porfirio Díaz, who ruled Mexico from 1876 to 1911, believed that Mexico's problems of disunity and poverty could be solved by "order and progress." His army supplied order by crushing those who disagreed. American and European businessmen supplied progress.

Progress meant railroads, better sanitation, telephone and telegraph lines, modern mining, oil drilling. Investment by foreign businessmen brought in money for public buildings and for paying off Mexico's foreign debt. But the vast majority of Mexicans remained as poor as they had ever been, while foreign investors and their Mexican allies grew richer.

By 1900 American companies like U.S. Steel and Standard Oil controlled about three-fourths of Mexico's mineral wealth. The British owned half the oil-bearing lands, Americans the rest. Foreign control meant that most Mexicans gained little from modernization. Railroads, for example, ran north from Mexico City into the United States, but not south into the rural country where they were needed.

Mexicans began to protest against Díaz's policies of "order and progress"—including his alliance with foreign businessmen. Some Americans supported the protests. American and Mexican workers alike were fighting for better wages and working conditions, often against the same companies. In the 1870s and 1880s American labor leaders visited Mexico to help railroad and textile workers set up unions to fight for better treatment.

The United States became a place of refuge for people who opposed Díaz. In the early 1900s the Flores Magón brothers fled north of the border. From their exile in St. Louis, Missouri, they called for liberal reform and the overthrow of Díaz. Local authorities arrested them on charges of breaking United States neutrality laws. But an outcry by the St. Louis press helped free them.

Still, for the most part, Mexicans who opposed Díaz saw the United States as an enemy. This view was strengthened by an incident in Cananea, a Mexican city near the border. There, in 1906, copper miners went on strike against their American employer, William Greene. They claimed that Greene paid them less than American workers and gave them lesser jobs. When violence flared up, Greene got permission from the Mexican governor to bring in 275 Arizona Rangers to suppress the strike. More than 200 people were killed.

Mexicans were shocked at the blood-

This American song from the 1860s protests the French intervention in Mexico.

shed in Cananea. They were outraged at their government for allowing American troops to intervene. Opposition to Díaz grew, and in November 1910, revolution rocked Mexico. The revolution went on for a decade. It established the Mexican constitution that exists today, but the price was paid in years of violence and turmoil.

During the revolution, American businesses came under attack. Revolutionary leaders wanted to drive foreign investors out of Mexico and give their property to the state. Mine owners saw their workers join the armies of such revolutionaries. Railroad owners saw miles of track destroyed. Rebel leader Pancho Villa seized cattle that belonged to millionaire William Randolph Hearst and sold them for arms.

Some people in the United States

Guerrilla leader Pancho Villa's 1916 raid on Columbus, New Mexico, led to U.S. intervention in the Mexican Revolution.

sided with the radical forces. Journalist John Reed marched with Pancho Villa and reported on his exploits in American newspapers. But the United States government feared radical forces. Washington wanted a government in Mexico that would maintain order and protect American holdings.

In pursuit of those goals, the United States intervened several times during the revolution, but with little lasting effect. American ambassador Henry Lane Wilson intervened through secret diplomacy. In a night meeting in February 1913, Wilson encouraged General Victoriano Huerta to seize power from the elected president of Mexico. Huerta did. But Woodrow Wilson, president of the United States, decided that Huerta could not protect American interests either.

In April 1914, the United States helped bring down Huerta's government. After a supposed insult to the American flag, U.S. naval forces captured the city of Veracruz as they had done 67 years earlier. Hundreds of Mexicans were killed, and supplies to

Huerta from the Gulf of Mexico were cut off. The occupation helped end the dictatorship, but it also raised a public outcry. The revolution went on, with greater hostility toward Americans.

The United States sent troops into Mexico once more during the revolution. This was in response to a raid by Pancho Villa's rebel soldiers. In 1916 the guerrillas crossed the border into New Mexico and killed eighteen people in the town of Columbus. President Wilson sent General John Pershing and 6,000 troops into northern Mexico to find and punish Villa. The "punitive expedition" clashed with Mexican troops but never found Villa.

The United States slowly learned that there were limits to what it could do in Mexico. In the revolution, and in the constitution of 1917, Mexico was finding its own identity as a nation. Relations with Mexico after the revolution gradually became warmer, but Mexico restricted the activities of foreign businesses and remained suspicious of the United States.

In 1933 President Franklin Roosevelt began "the Good Neighbor Policy" in Latin America. The United States avoided using armed force in the Western Hemisphere and increased peaceful cooperation.

In Mexico, the Good Neighbor Policy was tested in 1938 when President Lázaro Cárdenas nationalized the holdings of American oil companies, placing them under state ownership. Mexico took over the oilfields because, in a dispute with workers, the companies had refused to obey the Mexican Supreme Court. Mexicans cheered the action as a declaration of "economic independence." But some Americans called for the use of armed force.

President Roosevelt did not use armed force. The crisis was settled through diplomacy, with Mexico giving some payment to the oil companies for what they had lost. The United States had shown that it could be a fair neighbor, and Mexico more cooperative.

The benefits of cooperation were not always shared equally by both countries. The *bracero* program is an example. This program, begun in 1942, allowed Mexicans to work in the fields of U.S. growers for temporary periods. These *braceros*, or field workers, took the place of Americans drafted into the army during World War II. But growers wanted the program to continue after the war because it supplied them with inexpensive labor. Mexican *braceros* were treated poorly; Americans who wanted to work found themselves without jobs. Not until 1964 did the *bracero* program come to an end.

Since the 1950s the "Good Neighbor Policy" no longer exists in Latin America. The United States has returned to using armed force as one tool of its foreign policy in the Western Hemisphere. But against Mexico, at least, the United States has not used military force. Mexico remains an ally—as well as the third largest market for American goods.

The two countries have not forgotten that they were once enemies. Just as Texans still remember the Alamo, Mexicans remember *Los Niños Héroes*—the boy cadets who died fighting at Chapultepec. On March 18 of each year, they also celebrate the day of "economic in-dependence"—the day that American oilfields were nationalized for the benefit of Mexico.

Problems exist between Mexico and the United States. In the 1980s the United States protested against the flow of illegal drugs from Mexico, and also tried to stop the flow of Mexican "undocumented workers"—those who enter the United States illegally in search of employment. Undocumented workers who had been in the United States for more than four years were offered amnesty in 1986. The rest are facing stricter enforcement of immigration laws.

At home Mexico is facing an enormous burden of debt to other countries. In the years after World War II, Mexico's national oil industry brought new wealth to the country. In the 1970s loans from other countries and the discovery of new oilfields helped Mexico to grow. But the sharp drop in oil prices in the 1980s has made it hard for Mexico to pay back its debts to other countries, which had risen to over $100 billion by the end of the 1980s. Mexico has asked for help in dealing with its foreign debt—including relief from American banks.

In 1963 one boundary dispute still existed between the United States and Mexico. Both countries laid claim to 600 acres of land, called the Chamizal tract, near El Paso, Texas. The countries signed a treaty that divided the land between them. The piece of land was small, insignificant compared with what the two countries fought about in the 1840s. But the treaty showed that there are other ways to peace than war.

INDEX

Page numbers in *italics* indicate illustrations

SUGGESTED READING

ALBA, VICTOR. *The Horizon Concise History of Mexico*. New York: American Heritage, 1973.

MEIER, MATT S., and FELICIANO RIVERA. *The Chicanos: A History of Mexican Americans*. New York: Hill and Wang, 1972.

SINGLETARY, OTIS A. *The Mexican War*. Chicago: University of Chicago Press, 1960.

TINKLE, LON. *The Alamo*. New York: New American Library, 1958.